*THERE ARE ONLY TWO DAYS THAT
MATTER. THIS DAY AND THE DAY
YOU STAND BEFORE A HOLY GOD.
-MARTIN LUTHER*

Why the *21 Day Challenge*?

IF 1 PERSON DOES 1 THING
ONCE A DAY FOR 21 DAYS...
ONLY GOD KNOWS THE IMPACT
THAT CAN HAVE

THE
POWER
OF

Are you wondering why we need a *21 Day Challenge*?
The top 3 reasons are:

1. Desperate times call for desperate measures- Our world is in desperate shape. Christians are being persecuted across the globe and darkness is pressing in like never before. Watch the news if you don't agree then keep reading.

2. Lost people go to Hell- We must never forget this truth, Without Christ, people who die spend an eternity in a very real place called Hell. We have the antidote to the problem but we have to be willing to share it.

3. Obedience to the Great Commission-We will never be who God has called us to be if we are un willing to obey the Great Commission 'to go and make disciples.' It is not a suggestion-it is a commandment. We do not get to pick and choose which portions of Scripture we will obey.

Honestly, personal evangelism is a weak spot for many believers therefore it is an area that we need to be more intentional about strengthening. The world is becoming more and more aggressive while believers become more and more passive—its time for a change.

That means that we must become doers of the Word and not just hearers. No longer can we sit back in our comfortable houses and tune in to a sermon here and there while letting other people pick up the slack for us in reaching the world for Christ. It's time to start applying the things we have been learning.

When you complete this challenge, you will be more empowered to share your faith by telling your story, you will have a deeper relationship with Christ and you will have experienced the joy that comes from obedience in telling your story and most likely will also experience the joy that comes from leading someone to saving faith.

When we talk about telling your story you need to realize that it's more than a summary of your life—it's all about what God has done in and through you. By sharing your road to salvation as your story, it enables the person listening to connect with you quickly. People like to hear about others' lives and although that can be good, unless we are intentional about telling them the role Jesus has in our receiving forgiveness and redemption , then we are just entertaining them.

Throughout this *21 Day Challenge* we will be working on being more intentional about finding ways and times to tell people about Jesus and what he has done for us.

We may refer to this as sharing your faith, telling your story or witnessing but they all mean the same thing and they all have the same goal of reaching people with the gospel of Christ.

So if you are ready to stand up and be counted, to resign from ho hum Christianity and take your spiritual walk to a new level, then this is for you. We welcome you on this journey and pray that God will do amazing things in your life as you follow Him.

The Power of 1 is about the difference 1 person can make by doing 1 thing, once a day for 21 days. Once you have experienced what it is like to obey God by telling your story, then you will no longer be satisfied with sitting back and letting the world go to Hell all around you. This is life changing stuff. The challenge is here-the choice is yours.

The 21 Day Challenge is significant because it establishes a Biblical pattern or habit in your life of obedience in witnessing. It would be great if we jumped out of bed everyday with a heartfelt desire to share our faith, but unfortunately our flesh is weak. This kind of commitmen holds us accountable to surrender our day to the Holy Spirit and to look for the "divine appointments" He will have for us to share our faith.
-David Landrith, Pastor, Long Hollow Baptist Church

It takes 21 days to establish a habit, so this challenge covers 21 days.
DAILY ELEMENTS:

 WARM UP will start the day with Scripture.

 TRAINING SESSION gets you thinking about the topic of the day.

 WORKOUT designed to help you consider how the Word for the day applies directly to your life and what you can be doing differently.

 PERSONAL EVALUATION write the name of who you shared with that day. Write reflections on how the time went and anything you could have done differently. List any questions that may have come up and also take time to write out a prayer for the person.

Each element of each day is purposefully designed to help you complete this challenge, so don't skip over them. It is important to be intentional about who you are sharing with and to track the progress of your conversations.

PRACTICAL HELPS: Found at the back of this book. Included are such things as a worksheet to help organize your story. Some simple strategies you can use to lead someone to faith in Christ when they express interest. Thoughts from the perspective of a lost person. Memory verses and more.

ADDITIONAL RESOURCES: Go online and record some of your stories, ask questions and read about what God is doing through the *21 Day Challenge* everywhere at *www.takethe21daychallenge.wordpress.com.*

ACCOUNTABILITY: Find personal encouragement and support through small groups. If you have a group already, encourage them to join you on the challenge and take time to share with one another what God is doing. If you aren't involved in a small group, consider starting one yourself. Find 3 or 4 others and invite them to be part of this life changing adventure. This is your challenge so use it the way that best suits you.

TRAINING PHASE

1

THIS IS LOVE FOR GOD, TO OBEY HIS COMMANDS, AND HIS COMMANDS ARE NOT BURDENSOME, FOR EVERYONE BORN OF GOD OVERCOMES THE WORLD.
1 JOHN 5:3-4

TRAINING PHASE 1

OVERCOMING HURDLES

Physical fitness and weight loss strategies make up a huge portion of our economy today. One of the hardest things to do with these programs or regimens is to overcome the excuses and fears associated with making changes. The same is true of us spiritually. When we are faced with the Truth that we need to be more active in sharing our faith and living our lives so that we reflect Christ in every area, plenty of things will be there to tempt us away or hold us back—there will always be hurdles that we have to jump.

The first phase of the *21 Day Challenge* is focused on dealing with the things that hold us back and weigh us down to prevent us from being obedient to God. Growth is not always easy and becoming more healthy takes work, but it's worth it. A vital part of spiritual health and growth is the discipline of evangelism or telling your story of redemption and salvation. 1 Timothy 4:7-8 stresses the importance of spiritual fitness when it says *train yourself to be godly. For physical training is of some value, but godliness has value for all things, holding promise for both the present life and the life to come.* Another version ends with, *but godliness has value for all things for it yields a reward both in this life and the one to come.*

If you have ever been involved in some kind of exercise plan, then you are aware that pain and discomfort will often follow a tough workout. That can be comforting because the sore muscles let you know that you were working on the right things. It's a good reminder to us that if we want to train ourselves for spiritual godliness, then some pain and discomfort may result. We have to be willing to fight through the obstacles.

Too many times believers like us will consider telling people about Jesus or sharing about His love with others but then we let excuses quench the desire and we procrastinate until the opportunity has passed. This week you will be challenged to fight through the fears of telling your story. You will have the temptation to just lay this book aside and get back to it 'some other time'. There will be some crazy things happen when you begin to pray for God to show you who to share with. Be prepared and be intentional.

Everything may not go perfectly but don't give up. You have had the privilege of hearing about Jesus' work on the cross, will you really deny someone else the same because it is uncomfortable for you? Hell is a real place and when people die without Christ they spend eternity there. So focus on the end result and follow through. It will be oh so worth it!

MEASURING SUCCESS: In order to evaluate your progress along this challenge you'll need to understand how to measure success. Although it will be fantastic when people you share with choose to place their faith in Christ, for the purposes of the challenge we will define success by your obedience. Every time you obey God and share your story, count that as success! In sharing with the lost and unchurched you will likely have numerous opportunities to lead people to faith and that's great but if those same people aren't ready to accept Jesus then that doesn't mean you failed. Your obedience makes you a winner.

No discipline seems pleasant at the time, but painful. Later on, however, it produces a harvest of righteousness and peace for those who have been trained by it. Hebrews 12:11

DAY 1
IT AIN'T EASY

WARM UP   **Hebrews 12:1-2**

"Therefore, since we are surrounded by such a great cloud of witnesses, let us throw off everything that hinders and the sin that so easily entangles, and let us run with perseverance the race marked out for us. Let us fix our eyes on Jesus, the author and perfecter of our faith, who for the joy set before him endured the cross, scorning its shame, and sat down at the right hand of the throne of God."

TRAINING SESSION

"If it were easy, everyone would do it." Chances are you have heard someone say that. Especially if you're a fan of any heartwarming, yet mildly overdramatic, sports movie. While it may sound a bit cliché, there really is some powerful truth to it. Think about it. If getting a PhD were easy, everyone would do it. We all know it's not easy, which is why less than 1% of Americans have actually done it. The same goes for running a marathon, running for President, running into Target for "just a few minutes"—these things are tough to do, and that's why the vast majority of us don't do them!

So where does all this fit into our *21 Day Challenge*? It's no secret that one of the hardest things for most believers to do is share their faith. The reasons why are different for everyone. Many of us are just too fearful. We're afraid of not knowing what to say, not knowing how to say it, not knowing what they will say...you get the idea. Others of us may feel inadequate or unprepared. And some of us, if we were very honest, just don't care. There are many reasons why sharing your story isn't easy, but does that mean it's not worth doing? Definitely not!

If you're going to accept this challenge, it's time to follow the instructions from Hebrews and start throwing off all those things that "hinder" and "entangle." This week, we will explore in greater depth some of the hurdles and obstacles that keep us from sharing our story. Spend some time thinking and reflecting on what your personal hurdles are. Be honest. What's holding you back?

WORKOUT

What is something God has asked you to do in the past that was not easy, but that you were faithful to do?
What were the results of your obedience?
What are the specific struggles you face that keep you from sharing your story?

PRAYER

Pray and confess the times you allow fear or excuses to keep you from telling people about Jesus. Ask God to convict you before you give in and allow any obstacle to hinder you. Pray the words of Hebrews 12:1-2 for yourself, asking that the Lord would give you strength and endurance to run the race He has set before you.

PERSONAL EVALUATION

Today I shared with _____
My thoughts on how it went:
_____
_____
_____
_____

What I would do differently:
_____
_____
_____
_____

My prayer for this person:
_____
_____
_____
_____

1 Peter 3:14-15

But even if you should suffer for what is right, you are blessed. "Do not fear what they fear; do not be frightened." But in your hearts set apart Christ as Lord. Always be prepared to give an answer to everyone who asks you to give the reason for the hope that you have. But do this with gentleness and respect,

TRAINING SESSION

Have you ever been in a situation in which you could not fail? Not a "failure is not an option" type situation; but an instance where as long as you did something, whatever that something might be, you succeeded. An example might be running. If you run a 5K or on the rare occasion, a half marathon, and your personal goal is always just to cross the finish line then as long as you make it across, it's been a success. If you don't set your sights on a first place finish, then even when the hardcore runners are whizzing past you on their way back to the finish line as you approach mile one, that's okay. There's no pressure, no anxiety, and no fear of failure. Why? Because when it comes down to it, you can't fail! As long as you cross the finish line, no matter how long it takes you to get there, you've succeeded. The principle is still the same for other areas of life.. If you're doing something at which you know you cannot fail, there's really not much to be afraid of.

Think about this concept in terms of sharing your faith. Many Christians would admit that one of the biggest hurdles standing in their way is the fear of failure. Yet, the whole notion that sharing your faith is a pass or fail exercise is a lie from the Enemy.

It is one He uses to make evangelism a scary thing for many believers. If you view failure as not "doing it right" or not seeing the person you share with come to accept Christ, then yes, you'll often be crippled by fear. The best way to overcome this fear is to redefine your idea of failure and success in this area based on what God has to say. That way you can be freed up to obey without fear.

When does God consider us successful? Very simply, when we're obedient. Just like a proud dad who wraps his little boy in a hug after every game, no matter if he hit a home-run or never got the ball off the tee, our Daddy (God) is proud of us simply for stepping up to the plate. If He gives you an opportunity or causes you to feel like you should share your story of Christ's work on the cross with some-one, He's not going to hold you responsible for the out-come. That's His job, your job is just to obey Him when He prompts you or makes the opportunity available. You only have to answer for your obedience to complete the task He gives you. If you do that, you can't fail!

WORKOUT

How has a fear of failure or rejection ever kept you from sharing your story with someone else?
How does redefining your ideas about success and failure in this area, change the way you feel about sharing your story?

PRAYER

Pray that God will reveal to you your true fears. Confess those and ask His direction in developing your story or plan for sharing that will enable you to be prepared to 'give an account' of all he has done for you. Spend time thanking God for the work he is doing in your life.

PERSONAL EVALUATION

Today I shared with _____

My thoughts on how it went:

_____
_____
_____
_____

What I would do differently:

_____
_____
_____
_____

My prayer for this person:

_____
_____
_____
_____

WARM UP

Ephesians 5:15-16

"Be very careful, then, how you live-not as unwise but as wise, making the most of every opportunity, because the days are evil."

TRAINING SESSION

Not many feelings are more unpleasant than that of being unprepared. Sometimes, we find ourselves unprepared for something we knew was coming. Like April 15th rolls around and we're just getting the checkbook out. Oops. Other times, we're caught off guard by something that we had no way of preparing for—life's little pop quizzes, if you will. Whether the situation is major or minor, avoidable or unavoidable, being unprepared is frustrating.

When it comes to sharing our faith, many of us would say we don't feel truly prepared or ready to do it, and we use this as an excuse not to share. Well, speaking on the authority of the Scripture we read earlier, this excuse isn't good enough. Peter instructs believers to always be prepared *"to give the reason for the hope that you have."* This doesn't necessarily mean we need to have the book of Romans memorized and ready to spout off at a moment's notice. Instead, being prepared means we are daily—moment-by-moment—walking with Jesus in such a way that we're always ready to talk about him. His name is on the tip of our tongue because He is part of our everyday lives. Very simply, if our affection and attention are fixed on him, then we're ready.

There are some practical steps you can take to help overcome this fear of being unprepared to share your story. *For one thing, know your story.* Keep in mind, that it's not just the story of your life, like where you were born and how you got here today. It's the story of what Jesus has done for you by forgiving your sins and giving you a new life in Him. If you've never thought about how you would communicate what Christ has done in your life to another person, then *sitting down, thinking, and writing it out would be worth the time.* There is a simple worksheet on pages 84-85 that can help you organize your thoughts. It's also important to *be able to point people to appropriate Scripture when you're sharing your faith, so you may want to be committing some simple verse to memory or underlining them in your Bible so they stand out.* There are some great memory verses on pages 93-94 to get you started. And finally, *spend some time every morning asking God to prepare you for the opportunities He has for you that day.* He's got plans to use you in a big way, make sure you're ready.

WORKOUT

In what ways do you need to be more prepared to share your faith?
What steps then are you going to take to be ready to "make the most of every opportunity?"

PRAYER

Pray that God will direct as you write out your story and make a plan for sharing. Ask Him to increase your memory and help you to 'hide His word in your heart' (Ps.119:11).

NOTES:

PERSONAL EVALUATION

Today I shared with _____

My thoughts on how it went:

_____
_____
_____
_____

What I would do differently:

_____
_____
_____
_____

My prayer for this person:

_____
_____
_____
_____

WARM UP

Philippians 3:8

"What is more, I consider everything a loss compared to the surpassing greatness of knowing Christ Jesus my Lord, for whose sake I have lost all things. I consider them rubbish, that I may gain Christ."

1 Corinthians 1:18

"For the message of the cross is foolishness to those who are perishing, but to us who are being saved it is the power of God."

TRAINING SESSION

Have you ever thought about how much our culture values comfort? Americans, maybe more so than any other people in the world, go to great lengths to be comfortable. Exhibit A: the Snuggie. Not to pick on those of you wearing one as you read this, but let's be honest, the fact that we'll pay $25 for a backwards bathrobe so we don't have to expose our arms to flip the TV channel is kind of crazy. Seriously, we are a culture that craves comfort. The emphasis placed on comfort and ease spills right over into the area of relationships. In many of our relationships, we spend most of our time talking about nothing rather than something. We are all guilty, and it's not too hard to figure out why—talking about something of substance and value has the potential to create an uncomfortable situation. And who wants that?

In considering hurdles to overcome in sharing our faith, comfort is a big one. We fear the uncomfortable consequences that might come from a faith-centered conversation that doesn't go quite like we want it to. "What if

I talk to them about Christ and they get offended? "What if they think I'm judging them? "What if it changes our relationship?" "What if I actually push them farther away from God by trying to share with them?" What if they ask questions I can't answer? Many believers have allowed concerns like these to prevent them from having real conversations about their faith. Our lives are about comfort, and in trying to attain it, we manage to avoid talking about the one thing in life that really matters.

Understand that the real issue is not about the validity of your concerns. Honestly, some of these uncomfortable situations we've discussed might happen if you choose to share your faith. In 1 Corinthians, Paul pointed out that for some people, the message of the cross is "foolishness" and those that believe it may be seen as fools. Discomfort can happen. But the big question you must answer for yourself is this: Does my desire to be obedient to God's command and the possibility that this conversation could lead this person to a life-changing relationship with Jesus outweigh my concerns of creating an uncomfortable or awkward situation for the both of us? The answer to that question should be a resounding YES. And if it is, then let's start talking—talking about something.

There is a great tool for helping you understand how a lost person might react to certain things you say on page 96. Check it out and then get started talking to people about the One who can make an eternal difference to them.

WORKOUT

When was the last time you let fear of being uncomfortable keep you from talking about Jesus?

When you weigh the possibility of someone asking Christ into his or her heart against your fear, which is a stronger motivation?

Your fear of being uncomfortable is a form of selfishness—what will you do to obey rather than give in to selfishness?

PRAYER

Pray that God will make you more interested and concerned about lost people than you are about your own comfort.

PERSONAL EVALUATION

Today I shared with _____

My thoughts on how it went:

_____
_____
_____
_____

What I would do differently:

_____
_____
_____
_____

My prayer for this person:

_____
_____
_____
_____

WARM UP

Philippians 2:3-4

Do nothing out of selfish ambition or vain conceit. Rather, in humility value others above yourselves, not looking to your own interests but each of you to the interests of the others.

TRAINING SESSION

There is one day a year when most people expect to be the center of attention—their birthday. Others would rather their "big day" pass as uneventfully as possible. Regardless of how important or how insignificant birthdays are to you we're all guilty of forgetting someone else's birthday once in a while. Maybe we had good intentions of calling, writing, emailing, something… but for whatever reason, none of that happened. It's not that you don't care about them and it's not that they aren't important to you—it's just you got a little too distracted with your day to remember it was their day.

While remembering to wish someone a happy birthday is important, the constant state of distraction that some of us are in keeps us from carrying out tasks that are infinitely more important. For many overcommitted and stressed out Christians, the fact that we don't share our faith very much is not a result of being too afraid or feeling unprepared or inadequate. It's just that we're so caught up in everything going on in our own lives, that even unintentionally, evangelism just doesn't happen. We're guilty of doing exactly what Paul encouraged the believers in Philippi not to do, which is look to our own interests, considering them more important than the interests of anyone else. So we can call it being distracted or self-focused or any number of things, but the consequences are the same—lost people all around us die and go to Hell because we are too fixed on our own lives to notice and do anything about it.

The reason this **21 Day Challenge** can have such an incredible impact is because it's pushing us to get intentional about sharing our faith. For some, that's the biggest hurdle standing in the way. Yet, really it's one of the easiest ones to overcome! We start by committing it to prayer. Sounds simple, but constantly asking God to reset your focus on Him and other people, even on your busiest of days, makes a big difference. It might also help to write your lost friends' names on note cards and put them in places you'll see them all day. Finally, memorize and meditate on Scripture emphasizing that it's not all about us. You will find key memory verses in *Practical Helps*, pages 93-94 Make a point today to look up from your life and start living on purpose.

WORKOUT What are the biggest distractions in your day-to-day life that keep you from focusing on others?
What steps can you take to become more intentional about sharing your faith?

PRAYER Pray for God to give you a heart for the lost. Ask that the specific lost people you know already would be interested in spiritual things and for an opportunity to talk with them soon.

PERSONAL EVALUATION

Today I shared with _____

My thoughts on how it went:

_____
_____
_____
_____

What I would do differently:

_____
_____
_____
_____

My prayer for this person:

_____
_____
_____
_____

Romans 10:14-17

*Everyone who calls on the name of the Lord will be saved."
How, then, can they call on the one they have not believed
in? And how can they believe in the one of whom they
have not heard? And how can they hear without someone preaching to them? And how can anyone preach unless
they are sent? As it is written: "How beautiful are the feet
of those who bring good news!"*

TRAINING SESSION

Everybody needs a wake-up call from time to time.
I remember a time in college when I got a much-need-
ed wake-up call myself. It was my first semester at this
big state school and I was loving it. Between meeting
new people, getting to know new friends, going to
football games, and late night trips to the 24-hour Piz-
za Hut right next door—my days were full. After a few
weeks, the wake-up call came. My first big exam rolled
around. As you might have guessed, I didn't do so well.
It became abundantly clear that I needed to start focusing more on what I actually came to college to do. As
much as I (and my GPA) would've liked a do-over on
that first exam, that 'failure', was exactly what I needed.

Spiritually, we all need a wake-up call from time to
time. And there's probably no area that we need one
more urgently than in the area of sharing our faith. The
truth is, someof us don't have a major hurdle to overcome in sharing our story. It's not that we don't know
how or are afraid to do it. When it comes down to it,
we're just too apathetic about the whole thing. We've
forgotten what happens if we don'tshare. We look at
the lives of the lost people around and think, "Hey,
they're not doing so bad. It doesn't look like they're

really in desperate need for me to tell them about Jesus. If they want to talk about it, they'll ask." We're so focused on the visible and the outward appearance, that we're neglecting the unseen reality.

Recognizing that unseen reality is the only wake-up call we need. Scripture says it plainly, lost people go to Hell. They spend all of eternity separated from God in a place of torture and torment beyond our understanding. (Revelation 14:9-11). Yet, even though we know this to be true, we can remain unmoved by it if we continue to think of lost people as nameless, faceless group, to whom we have no personal attachment. We have to recognize that the lost are own brothers, next-door neighbors, and best friends, who are destined for an eternity in Hell if they don't know Jesus. Are we okay with that? Hopefully not—and there's our wake-up call.

WORKOUT

Someone once said "They used to be apathetic and now they just don't care". Whatever you call it, the reality is that too many believers aren't concerned about the fate of lost people. On a scale of 1-10 with 1 being "who cares" and 10 being "I'm overcome with the weight of the lost", where do you fall on the scale? How have you become so apathetic?

Look up the word Hell in your concordance or use an online tool to read more about that very real place. Does that in any way motivate you to move away from being focused on yourself enough to share with others? Do so.

PRAYER

Pray for forgiveness for your lack of love and concern for others. Ask the Lord to help you care more about your neighbor than you do yourself.

**PERSONAL
EVALUATION**

Today I shared with _____

My thoughts on how it went:

_____
_____
_____
_____

What I would do differently:

_____
_____
_____
_____

My prayer for this person:

_____
_____
_____
_____

Romans 10:14-17

As Jesus was getting into the boat, the man who had been demon-possessed begged to go with him. Jesus did not let him, but said, "Go home to your own people and tell them how much the Lord has done for you, and how he has had mercy on you." So the man went away and began to tell in the Decapolis[a] how much Jesus had done for him. And all the people were amazed.

TRAINING SESSION

Have you ever managed to get out of doing something, because you weren't very good at it? For instance, maybe you're a notoriously bad driver. This doesn't really come in handy until the family road trip rolls around and you get to snooze for 12 straight hours in the back because no one would dare let you take a turn in the driver's seat. On such rare occasions, being "challenged" in a certain area has its perks. Most of the time, however, despite our lack of ability in an area, we just have to step up and do it. Saying "it's not my thing" just won't cut it.

From time to time, we're guilty of using this excuse when it comes to evangelism. You've probably heard someone say, or maybe you've said it yourself, that evangelism "just isn't my thing. It's not my gift, and it's probably better left to someone who is gifted in that particular area." It might be true that some people are more gifted in the area of sharing their faith, that it comes a little easier to them than to others. Yet the truth is that any person, whose sins have been forgiven and whose eternity has been secured through faith in Jesus, is called and capable of telling others what God's done in his or her life.

See
PRACTICAL
HELPS:
*Identifying Lost
People, p.*

We've used the old excuse that, "somebody else will do it" for far too long. There are people in your life that you have been divinely placed with, either by birth or by choice, that don't know Christ. And no one can tell them your story but you. What did Jesus instruct the demon-possessed man to do after he was healed? He didn't tell him to go find an evangelist to tell his story to everyone else. He told the man that it was his job to go tell his friends what the Lord had done in his life. Out of the overflow of what Christ has done for him, he shared his story. Has your life been changed by Christ? Then you're called to do the same.

WORKOUT

Is evangelism your spiritual gift? If not, do you know what your spiritual gifts are? Check out an on-line evaluation to help you discover the way you've been gifted. (www.longhollow.com/serve/spiritualgifts) Whatever ways you are gifted or talented can be used by God to share His love with others. List some things you are good at or that you like to do. You don't have to share Jesus like a preacher or an evangelist would, you just have to share Jesus like only you can.

PRAYER

Pray that God will show you how He wants you to use your gifts to share Him with others. Ask for courage to step out in faith as you obey Him today.

PERSONAL EVALUATION

Today I shared with _____

My thoughts on how it went:

_____
_____
_____
_____

What I would do differently:

_____
_____
_____
_____

My prayer for this person:

_____
_____
_____
_____

NOTES

TRAINING PHASE

2

FOR GOD HATH NOT GIVEN
US THE SPIRIT OF FEAR,
BUT OF POWER, AND OF LOVE,
AND OF A SOUND MIND.
2 TIMOTHY 1:7

TRAINING PHASE 2

POWER UP

As we move into the next week of the challenge, it's time to focus on strength training. When you want to build your physical muscles then you actually have to work them so hard that you break the muscle down. Then it will be able to build back stronger than before. It seems crazy but in reality you have to tear down to build up.

That is exactly what we are in the process of doing spiritually. We are tearing down our reliance on ourselves and our excuses and we are building up our reliance on God and His power. After dealing with the various excuses and hindrances that we have become so comfortable with in the past, we are now going to focus our attention on spiritual strength building.

These next several days will be pushing us to lift some heavier weight spiritually. We will study Scriptures that teach about the power of God and intentionally seek that power for our own lives as we continue to share our stories. Remember that it is by challenging and pushing ourselves that we are able to gain that next level both physically and spiritually. So don't back down and don't even think about giving up---no matter how the past few days have gone for you. Whether you feel like a success or not, choose now to be obedient and you will be blessed for that. His Word promises it!

Look at what Acts 1:8 says *"But you will receive power when the Holy Spirit comes on you; and you will be my witnesses in Jerusalem, and in all Judea and Samaria, and to the ends of the earth."*

Here's a cool thing about the power that we are told we can receive. It's a greek word "dynamis" and it means "strength, power and ability, which is what you would think, but there is more to the word. It also means "power for performing miracles." Don't miss that. This is big power we are talking about. It is also the same word that is used for the power that raised Jesus from the dead.

Another place this same word for power is found is in 2 Timothy 1:7 *"For God did not give us a spirit of timidity, but a spirit of power, of love and of self-discipline."*

Remember, no matter what tries to interfere with you sharing, or what hinders you, you have power that is stronger and greater than anything else at your disposal. Use it!

WARM UP

Romans 15:13

"May the God of hope fill you with all joy and peace as you trust in him, so that you may overflow with hope by the power of the Holy Spirit."

TRAINING SESSION

As you have been sharing about Christ and the difference He can make, you might have experienced some helpless or frustrating feelings. Many times this results when you do everything you can think of and yet nothing seems to be happening with the other person. Sometimes this can be a result of relying on our own strength and power instead of on God's power that is available for each of us.

Romans 15:13 is a great prayer to use as you prepare to share with others. Get in the habit of asking the Lord to fill you with His Spirit so that you overflow with hope and peace, not frustration. Realize that your responsibility is to share the gospel and to do that most effectively, you need to be living in the power of the Holy Spirit not just trusting in your own strength. Also important to understand is that it is the work of the Holy Spirit that actually saves people. In other words, do your job and trust the Spirit of God to do His. Every believer has the opportunity to live surrendered to the Spirit every day. If you are willing to give Him control then you will be amazed at all He can do in and through you.

WORKOUT

If you aren't living full of the Holy Spirit, what is filling you in His place? (need to make money, fear, stress, striving for perfection…)
Why is it dangerous to live depending on your own strength and power?
What areas of your life do you try to keep control over?

PRAYER

Pray that God will give you a hunger and thirst for Him. Use the words from Psalm 63:1 to express your need for God. Ask that He make you aware of the things that you are filling your life with other than the Holy Spirit and pray for wisdom to make the necessary changes.

PERSONAL EVALUATION

Today I shared with _____

My thoughts on how it went:

_____
_____
_____
_____

What I would do differently:

_____
_____
_____
_____

My prayer for this person:

_____
_____
_____
_____

DAY 9
TEST YOURSELF

WARM UP

2 Cor. 13:4-5

"For to be sure, He (Christ)was crucified in weakness, yet He lives by God's power. Likewise, we are weak in him, yet by God's power we will live with him to serve you. Examine yourselves to see whether you are in the faith; test yourselves. Do you not realize that Christ Jesus is in you-unless, of course, you fail the test?"

TRAINING SESSION

There are times in training or performing when you might need what is called an old fashioined 'gut check'. That typically means that you evaluate where you are and where you want to be then determine if you have the 'guts' to stick with it to the finish. Have you had a spiritual gut check lately? Today's Scripture gives the instruction to 'test' yourself to see whether you are in the faith or not.

It's entirely possible to have a desire to live for Christ and even the knowledge of how to do that but not actually be living in His power. There is a vast difference between head knowledge of Jesus and a personal relationship with Him. If you have been struggling with what to say to people about Christ or even being motivated to do this challenge then test yourself by answering the Workout questions honestly.

WORKOUT

Can you clearly remember a time when you recognized your sin and need for a Savior, then asked Jesus into your heart?

If you don't feel certain of your personal relationship with Jesus, take a few minutes to pray and ask that the Lord reveal truth to you. If necessary, turn to pages 88-91 and read through a plan of salvation to help determine if that is something that you've done or not. If no, -trust Him today. Record your decision to accept Christ and let someone in your accountability or small group know!

If you do have an assurance of your salvation then praise God for His free gift of salvation and consider where you would have been without Him.

PRAYER

Pray for a passion to see other people come to saving faith in Christ.

PERSONAL EVALUATION

Today I shared with _____

My thoughts on how it went:

_____

_____

_____

_____

What I would do differently:

_____

_____

_____

_____

My prayer for this person:

_____

_____

_____

WARM UP

Acts 4:13

"When they saw the courage of Peter and John and realized that they were unschooled, ordinary men, they were astonished and they took note that these men had been with Jesus."

TRAINING SESSION

When was the last time you saw someone and knew what they had been doing? Maybe you can tell someone has been working out by their clothing or their gym bag. Someone you work with may have just had an unpleasant meeting with the boss and you can tell by the look on his or her face. It's interesting to notice that when people saw the courage of Peter and John it was obvious these guys had been with Jesus.

Get this. Even though you may feel inadequate or unworthy of the task God has given you, what was true of Peter and John is also true for you. He will supply the power you need to fulfill the tasks He gives you. The key is take the time to be with the Father first. People will notice the difference and so will you.

WORKOUT

How do you notice the difference in yourself when you take time with God daily?

What are you doing to make that time alone with God a priority?

Identify what keeps you from making time alone with God what it should be.

PRAYER

Pray that the Lord will help you trust in His power and seek after it. Ask for guidance as you set aside time daily to meet with Him and commit to making that time a priority.

PERSONAL EVALUATION

Today I shared with _____

My thoughts on how it went:

_____

_____

_____

_____

What I would do differently:

_____

_____

_____

_____

My prayer for this person:

_____

_____

_____

_____

2 Corinthians 10:4-5

"For though we live in the world, we do not wage war as the world does. The weapons we fight with are not the weapons of the world. On the contrary, they have divine power to demolish strongholds. We demolish arguments and every pretension that sets itself up against the knowledge of God, and we take captive every thought to make it obedient to Christ."

TRAINING SESSION

These past few days we have been focused on building strength and living in the power of the Holy Spirit. Today's verses remind us why power is so important to the believer. It's because we are in a war. Don't minimize this. This war is not like one of those little arguments that happen when you were young and someone took your toy so you shoved them. This war is about the fate of souls for eternity.

In case you haven't thought it through very well, that's what this entire challenge is about. Lost people go to Hell when they die. Unless we help them recognize their need for a Savior and they ask Jesus into their hearts, that's exactly what will happen. The war is because the Enemy (Satan) is very determined to keep people from choosing Christ.

Some good news is found in 2 Corinthians. Our weapons for the spiritual war we find ourselves in are not of this world and they have divine power, there's that word again. In essence we can be assured that when we arm ourselves according to God's Word His power is strong enough to tear down the strongholds that keep people from the life God has for them.

WORKOUT

What are some ways that you can arm yourself with the weapons of God?

How have you seen the power of God tear down strongholds in your life?

What are some strongholds you have seen that need to be removed as you have been sharing with others?

Are there any thoughts you have been entertaining that need to be taken captive by the knowledge of God?

PRAYER

Ask God to show you any potential stongholds. Thank Him for loving you enough to fight with you on your behalf.

PERSONAL EVALUATION

Today I shared with _____

My thoughts on how it went:

_____
_____
_____
_____

What I would do differently:

_____
_____
_____
_____

My prayer for this person:

_____
_____
_____
_____

WARM UP

2 Peter 1:3

"His divine power has given us everything we need for life and godliness through our knowledge of him who called us by his own glory and goodness. Through these he has given us his very great and precious promises, so that through them you may participate in the divine nature and escape the corruption in the world caused by evil desires. For this very reason, make every effort to add to your faith goodness; and to goodness, knowledge; and to knowledge, self-control; and to self-control, perseverance; and to perseverance, godliness and to godliness, brotherly kindness; and to brotherly kindness, love. For if you possess these qualities in increasing measure, they will keep you from being ineffective and unproductive in your knowledge of our Lord Jesus Christ."

TRAINING SESSION

When you are on a quest to get fit and increase strength, one of the most frustrating things is when you work out hard, eat less, etc. and no progress is evident. We struggle when we feel like we are unproductive or ineffective. This is also true of our efforts at the *21 Day Challenge*.

The cool thing is that God knew we would have trouble with this. He used Peter to write words of encouragement for us when we tend to get discouraged, or feel ineffective. Look at what is said about His divine power in our lives. Do you really get that you have everything you need for life and godliness? Have you ever gotten caught up in thinking that there is something more you need to acquire or some type of penance you must do in order to receive His power? Even though there are no legalistic hoops you have to jump through, there are some things you need to be working on adding to your life.

WORKOUT

What from the list in 2 Peter do you most need to be adding to your life?
How can you go about increasing these qualities?

PRAYER

Thank the Lord that He has promised to give you the power you need for godliness. Thank Him that there is nothing you can do apart from Him to achieve godliness.

PERSONAL EVALUATION

Today I shared with _____

My thoughts on how it went:
_____
_____
_____
_____

What I would do differently:
_____
_____
_____
_____

My prayer for this person:
_____
_____
_____
_____

2 Kings 6:15-17

When the servant of the man of God got up and went out early the next morning, an army with horses and chariots had surrounded the city. "Oh, my lord, what shall we do?" the servant asked. "Don't be afraid," the prophet answered. "Those who are with us are more than those who are with them." And Elisha prayed, "O Lord, open his eyes so he may see." Then the Lord opened the servant's eyes, and he looked and saw the hills full of horses and chariots of fire all around Elisha.

TRAINING SESSION

War is not a new thing for Christ followers. In Elisha's day there was a pretty big battle happening and some of his men, including his own servant, were getting worried about their odds against the larger more powerful looking enemy. Notice what Elisha asked of God and what happened.

When the servant was able to see all of the armies the Lord had for their side, victory seemed much more attainable and he was reassured. Although our war is not being waged on the literal battlefield in most cases, it is still a very real battle. Have you experienced anything that reassured you God is on your side and He is fighting the battle with you and through you? If you are at a place where you feel like reinforcements would be helpful, pray and ask God to send help your way then watch for it. He is always at work around us—we just need to open our eyes.

WORKOUT

What is your toughest battle right now?
Are you trusting that you aren't alone?
What ways have you seen God at work around you recently?

PRAYER

Praise God for being on your side. Praise Him for the mighty ways that He protects you and loves you. Ask Him to reveal the sources of help that He has positioned in your life.

PERSONAL EVALUATION

Today I shared with _____

My thoughts on how it went:

_____
_____
_____
_____

What I would do differently:

_____
_____
_____
_____

My prayer for this person:

_____
_____
_____
_____

WARM UP

Deut 31:6-8

"Be strong and courageous. Do not be afraid or terrified because of them, for the Lord your God goes with you; he will never leave you nor forsake you." Then Moses summoned Joshua and said to him in the presence of all Israel, "Be strong and courageous, for you must go with this people into the land that the Lord swore to their forefathers to give them, and you must divide it among them as their inheritance. The Lord himself goes before you and will be with you; he will never leave you nor forsake you. Do not be afraid; do not be discouraged."

TRAINING SESSION

At this point in the 21 Day Challenge, you may be extremely pumped up or you could be getting discouraged. Either way, take heart in the verses for today. If you are fired up and excited about all God is doing through your obedience then continue on and be ready for the next opportunity and the next 'land' that God has for you to take. Just as the Israelites had to trust and follow the Lord into the promised land, you must do the same. Be ready to branch out and explore new territories of sharing your faith.

If you're struggling with some aspect of this challenge then "be strong and courageous" because you are not alone and God is going before you and will be with you. You can trust Him and that will never be more evident than as you tell your story about His work in your life.

WORKOUT

Where are you on this journey of faith? Just starting out? Stuggling to keep going? Pressing on?
What do you need strength or courage for right now? Personally? In your family? At your work/school?

PRAYER

Thank the Lord for being in your life and giving you the strength and power you need for every situation in your life. Commit to trusting in Him regardless of what your circumstances may be saying.

PERSONAL EVALUATION

Today I shared with _____

My thoughts on how it went:

_____
_____
_____
_____

What I would do differently:

_____
_____
_____
_____

My prayer for this person:

_____
_____
_____
_____

NOTES

TRAINING PHASE

3

BE WISE IN THE WAY YOU
ACT TOWARD OUTSIDERS,
MAKING THE MOST OF
EVERY OPPORTUNITY.
COLOSSIANS 4:5

TRAINING PHASE 3

IT'S TIME

You're doing great! You've probably had an interesting two weeks of sharing your story and have surely learned a lot in the process. After dealing with things that hinder us, then focusing on tapping into the power that's available, it's time to turn it up another notch.

For the next few days, we need to consider the way we spend our time in relationship to our spiritual lives. Often when you begin a new regimen it can be hard to find the time to squeeze anything else into your busy schedule. You may have even struggled to fit in time to share your story with people these past two weeks. It's time to change the way we think about time. Athletes wear watches that have the capacity to measure their pulse, heart rate, interval times and much more. The type of watch competitors wear can say a lot about their dedication to their training. The way we spend and measure our time says a lot about what we consider important.

Martin Luther once said, "There are only two days that matter, *this* day and the day you stand before a Holy God". The truth of this statement is our inspiration and motivation for *Training Phase 3*. We must become more intentional about the way we spend our time today so that when we must give an account for our lives, we will not be ashamed or embarrassed. As Christ followers, we need to have a healthy 'fear of the Lord' and of *that* day, which should motivate us to spend our days more wisely.

Consider this. There are 2 main Greek words used for time in the New testament; chronos and kairos. The first, chronos, indicates the literal passing of time as in minute by minute. The second word is kairos and it's the one you need to understand better. Although it is often translated as 'time' the word kairos is also translated as 'opportunity' such as in Ephesians 5:15-16 "Be very careful, then, how you live-not as unwise but as wise, making the most of every *opportunity*, because the days are evil." Check out the definition of 'kairos' below:

1) due measure, 2) a measure of time, a larger or smaller portion of time, hence: a) a fixed and definite time, the time when things are brought to crisis, the decisive epoch waited for b) opportune or seasonable time c) the right time d) a limited period of time

Did you catch the difference? Some commentaries point out that 'kairos' is used when making the distinction between the literal minutes on the clock and the *God ordained* moments in your day. Big difference. We have all been guilty of wishing for more minutes in our days. The truth is that we will only ever have 1,440 minutes in a day and we probably don't waste too many. But on the flip side, how many God-ordained moments have you been guilty of missing because you were too focused on the literal minutes in your day. Have you ever been hurrying through the grocery and seen someone you knew but because your schedule was so tight that day, you avoided her even though you could tell it was a bad day for her and she might need an encouraging word? Has a co-worker ever looked like they needed some encouragement, but you avoided them because you were too tired thinking about your own issues? Not a proud moment for a Christ follower. But a great example of how we get so focused on the *chronos* in our lives that we tend to miss out on the *kairos* moments and those are the ones where life change happens.

These next few days will offer some different examples to help us learn how to make the most of every opportunity we are given. As you read these stories and situations from the Word, take note of what you can draw from them and apply to your own life so that you become a person who doesn't have regrets about the way you treat the *kairos* that come your way. Remember, how you spend this day will greatly affect the day you stand before a Holy God. Use it wisely.

WARM UP

Acts 13:16

"Be strong and courageous. Do not be afraid or terrified because of them, for the Lord your God goes with you; he will never leave you nor forsake you." Then Moses summoned Joshua and said to him in the presence of all Israel, "Be strong and courageous, for you must go with this people into the land that the Lord swore to their forefathers to give them, and you must divide it among them as their inheritance. The Lord himself goes before you and will be with you; he will never leave you nor forsake you. Do not be afraid; do not be discouraged."

TRAINING SESSION

Paul, one of the most powerful Christian influences of all times, offers several examples of how to connect your audience with the message of the gospel. One great way to do this is to start with something familiar to the other person. Paul knew that the people he was speaking to were in the habit of telling stories of generations past so he started by doing the same thing. He recounted God's presence with their ancestors and engaged his listeners in the story. If you continue reading this passage, you will see how he brings them from back when their ancestors were enslaved in Egypt to their current day.

When you find common ground with the person you are sharing with, then the feeling becomes more of a 'we' than a 'you' atmosphere and that can prevent them from feeling defensive. When someone feels like they are connected to you in some way, they will usually be more open to hearing about how much Jesus loves them also. See pages 86-87 for some specific conversation starters that can help make this a common practice for you.

WORKOUT

What is your most effective tool to connect with someone? What have you learned from today's example that you can put into practice?

List any questions you have about this concept of connecting and discuss them in your small group or online.

PRAYER

Ask God to show you the common ground you have with others. Ask Him to give you the courage to start conversations with the tools you are acquiring in the *21 Day Challenge*.

PERSONAL EVALUATION

Today I shared with _____

My thoughts on how it went:

_____
_____
_____
_____

What I would do differently:

_____
_____
_____

My prayer for this person:

_____
_____
_____
_____

WARM UP

Matthew 26:7

"a woman came to him(Jesus) with an alabaster jar of very expensive perfume, which she poured on his head as he was reclining at the table. When the disciples saw this, they were indignant. "Why this waste?" they asked. "This perfume could have been sold at a high price and the money given to the poor." Aware of this, Jesus said to them, "Why are you bothering this woman? She has done a beautiful thing to me. The poor you will always have with you, but you will not always have me When she poured this perfume on my body, she did it to prepare me for burial. I tell you the truth, wherever this gospel is preached throughout the world, what she has done will also be told, in memory of her.""

TRAINING SESSION

As you have been sharing your story and talking about Jesus, you've probably been drawing some negative comments from others. Just as the woman who came to see and worship Jesus, when you step out in obedience there will almost always be people who ridicule and criticize. Why? They don't get it. They may even feel threatened by your spiritual growth. Some will be jealous that you are developing a more passionate relationship with Christ. The fact is that when you get serious about obeying God, then persecution will come in some way so be ready.

How do you continue in what you know to do when others give you a hard time? You focus on who you worship and who you follow. Jesus. When your eyes are fixed on Him then those around you will fade into the background and maybe at some point they will even be interested in hearing your story. Face it, the world doesn't like it when believers start living lives that glorify God so think of any opposition you encounter as positive reinforcement that you're on the right track. The woman braved the scorn of a powerful group of men to get to Jesus, can we do anything less?

WORKOUT

When was the most recent time someone has made fun of or put you down for talking about Jesus?
What has been your response when that happens?
How does the story of the woman with the alabaster jar encourage you to be bold in sharing Jesus?

PRAYER

Thank God that we live in a country where we are allowed to talk about Him without fear for our lives. Ask Him to encourage you when you are fearful of being mocked. Ask Him to remind you of the cost He paid for you.

PERSONAL EVALUATION

Today I shared with _____

My thoughts on how it went:

_____
_____
_____
_____

What I would do differently:

_____
_____
_____
_____

My prayer for this person:

_____
_____
_____
_____

WARM UP   Acts 8:27

"Now an angel of the Lord said to Philip, 'Go south to the road-the desert road-that goes down from Jerusalem to Gaza.' So he started out, and on his way he met an Ethiopian eunuch, an important official in charge of all the treasury of Candace, queen of the Ethiopians. This man had gone to Jerusalem to worship, and on his way home was sitting in his chariot reading the book of Isaiah the prophet. The Spirit told Philip, 'Go to that chariot and stay near it. Then Philip ran up to the chariot and heard the man reading Isaiah the prophet. 'Do you understand what you are reading?' Philip asked."

TRAINING SESSION

This is one of the coolest stories of a 'kairos' moment. Philip was right where he needed to be in order to 'happen' onto the Ethiopian reading God's Word. Hopefully you realize that this was no accident and that the God of the Universe completely orchestrated these events. It's also wise to recognize that Philip was not a puppet. He had the responsibility to obey and go where God wanted him to go. Did you catch how Philip responded when the angel spoke to him? "So he started out..." That definitely implies immediate obedience. God instructed and he went. No questions asked. No bargaining or deal making was going on. He just started out.

We have a crucial lesson to learn from Philip in this story. When God sends us a certain direction—we must go. The way that these 'kairos' moments happen most effectively is when the people of God respond to Him right away. Imagine what would have happened if Philip had first run home to pack a bag or change shoes or stop by the office first. What if he had kept asking the angel questions like "what am I supposed to do on that road?" "why do I need to go now". Philip could have reasoned with God that maybe there was a better route to get to the final destination than the one he mentioned. If he had been concerned about understanding all the details then he very well may have missed the opportunity to speak to the Ethiopian and subsequently lead him to faith and then baptize him! Our job is trust and follow the directions as God gives them.

WORKOUT

What is your usual response to instruction from the Lord? Do you obey or is your obedience tied to your understanding of the situation?

Have you ever tried to reorganize God and missed out on a big blessing? (Maybe avoided sharing with someone or going on a certain mission trip that you knew God was calling you to?)

What do you need to do differently to be prepared to trust and follow God step by step?

PRAYER

Pray that you will be more trusting when God does direct your path. Ask Him to orchestrate 'kairos' moments in your life today. Commit to obeying and following Him each step of the way and confess your obsession with knowing all the details before you'll obey.

**PERSONAL
EVALUATION**

Today I shared with _____

My thoughts on how it went:

_____
_____
_____
_____

What I would do differently:

_____
_____
_____
_____

My prayer for this person:

_____
_____
_____
_____

DAY 18
GO WITH WHAT YOU KNOW

WARM UP **Acts 15:12**

"The whole assembly became silent as they listened to Barnabas and Paul telling about the miraculous signs and wonders God had done among the Gentiles through them."

TRAINING SESSION

Who is more persuasive? Someone who sort of knows about something or someone who is passionate about something because he or she has experienced it? Well duh, the one who is passionate about and who has experiential knowledge will be more influential.

Look at how Paul and Barnabas spoke to their audience. They told about the miraculous signs and wonders that they had been part of. You don't have to know about everyone else's story of forgiveness and salvation, you just have to be willing to share yours. In order to be effective in making the most of your time, learn to go with what you know. Use the worksheet on pages 84-85 to organize your thoughts and remember that you don't have to try and tell about Jesus the exact way someone else would. Share what you know about what He has done in your life. That will make all the difference.

WORKOUT

What are some specific miracles that you have seen God do in your life? (remember salvation is a miracle as are changed lives and attitudes)

How would you rate yourself on a persuasive scale?

Do you come across as excited about Christ and the difference He makes or not?

What can you change to be more persuasive?

PRAYER

Our God is a passsionate God who is jealous for your devotion. Ask Him to ignite a fire in you for His people. Ask Him to make you passionately in love with Him.

PERSONAL EVALUATION

Today I shared with _____

My thoughts on how it went:

_____
_____
_____
_____

What I would do differently:

_____
_____
_____
_____

My prayer for this person:

_____
_____
_____
_____

WARM UP

Daniel 1

At the end of the ten days they looked healthier and better nourished than any of the young men who ate the royal food. So the guard took away their choice food and the wine they were to drink and gave them vegetables instead. To these four young men God gave knowledge and understanding of all kinds of literature and learning. And Daniel could understand visions and dreams of all kinds. At the end of the time set by the king to bring them in, the chief official presented them to Nebuchadnezzar. The king talked with them, and he found none equal to Daniel, Hananiah, Mishael and Azariah; so they entered the king's service

TRAINING SESSION

The world watches people who say they follow Christ to see if they really mean it. Why? Because too many claim to be believers and yet look, act , dress, talk and live just like the lost world. Daniel and his friends were taken into captivity and told to eat certain foods that were against their faith practices at the time, so they respectfully requested not to. They didn't just risk ridicule for their faith, they faced death and they chose to stand out for the Lord anyway.

Believers today get so caught up in keeping up with their neighbors, getting ahead at work, making the right friends and looking as much like media says we should look that too many of us are not being recognized as who's we really are. If you want to take your faith to another level, live in such obedience to God that people notice. You won't even have to start conversations about Jesus because people will ask you to tell them why you seem different. The cool thing about that is they will be even more interested because they have heard your story and they will have seen your faith in the way you live your life.

WORKOUT

When you consider the way you live, would you say that you stand out or blend in?

What are some things you avoid doing in obedience to God because of what someone might say?

How does Daniel's story challenge those attitudes that yell at you to blend in and not be different?

PRAYER

Pray that you will be much more interested in obedience to God than you are in what other people say about you. Ask the Lord to give you strength to stand out and be noticed and then when people ask why you're different to have the words to tell them who Jesus is in your life.

PERSONAL EVALUATION

Today I shared with _____

My thoughts on how it went:

_____
_____
_____
_____

What I would do differently:

_____
_____
_____
_____

My prayer for this person:

_____
_____
_____
_____

WARM UP

Acts 16:9

"During the night Paul had a vision of a man of Macedonia standing and begging him, "Come over to Macedonia and help us." After Paul had seen the vision, we got ready at once to leave for Macedonia, concluding that God had called us to preach the gospel to them."

TRAINING SESSION

Another great characteristic that Paul demonstrates is that of immediate obedience. "At once" is the way he responded to God's call. How often do you respond that way? We are typically so busy and our schedules are so full that if God were to say 'go talk to that person about me', it would take a convention between our iPad, laptop, iPhone, cell phone and blackberry to get time arranged and then we would still have to be making other calls and taking text messages while we were there. With the crazy calendars we keep, by the time we can squeeze someone new in the moment would most likely be gone. How prepared are you to respond to God with immediate obedience?

Anne Graham Lotz once shared that she always blocks off chunks of time in her schedule so that when the Lord brings some unexpected encounters her way, she has plenty of time to do whatever He asks. Do you fill your calendar and then ask the Lord to bless it or do you ask the Lord to fill your calendar? Too many of us use our busy lives as an excuse not to obey God. We tell Him and ourselves, "When things settle down I'll...." That's not the kind of obedience God desires or deserves. Delayed obedience is disobedience.

WORKOUT

Would you classify yourself as more immediately obedient or delayed obedient?

How will you make changes necessary to be prepared to obey God and take advantage of the 'kairos' moments?

PRAYER

Pray and ask God to change your attitude about your schedule and to give you a desire to let Him fill your days with what pleases Him. Confess any areas of disobedience and pray for wisdom to see where and how to make changes.

PERSONAL EVALUATION

Today I shared with _____

My thoughts on how it went:

_____
_____
_____
_____

What I would do differently:

_____
_____
_____
_____

My prayer for this person:

_____
_____
_____
_____

WARM UP

Acts 13:42

As Paul and Barnabas were leaving the synagogue, the people invited them to speak further about these things on the next Sabbath. When the congregation was dismissed, many of the Jews and devout converts to Judaism followed Paul and Barnabas, who talked with them and urged them to continue in the grace of God. On the next Sabbath almost the whole city gathered to hear the word of the Lord.

TRAINING SESSION

If someone you know was about to sink a lot of money into something that you knew was a scam, wouldn't you want them to know the truth about it? There is a great temptation, when talking to people about faith, to agree with their beliefs (whether right or wrong) and affirm them in how they were raised or whatever. But what if they are putting their faith in something that is contrary to Scripture? The consequences of that are much worse than just losing a lot of money or being embarrassed financially—this is eternity we're talking about. It's imperative that we learn to overcome our desire to be liked by everyone and not ever stand for something that may not be popular.

Look at what Paul and Barnabas did. They went and spoke the truth to a group of people who had some reason to be resistant. Notice the results. The next week, even more people were present to hear more truth. That's what can happen when we share the Truth of God's Word with others. They are attracted to it and will want to know more, usually. If not, then you have still been obedient to speak truth and the responsibility for how they respond is theirs.

There are some things you can be intentional about that will help people be more willing to hear Truth. Understand that the message is huge but so is the method that you use. Speaking the truth must be done in love, not as an attack. With a humble spirit and not a condemning attitude. From a caring heart not an argumentative spirit. Although this may sound tough, in reality If you continue to seek the

opportunities that God brings your way and make your own spiritual preparation a priority, then you'll be speaking the truth in love and people will be more receptive.

WORKOUT

When have you been guilty of using the Truth in a condemning or antagonistic way?
Do you tend to give in to the opinions of others in order to 'just get along'?

PRAYER

Pray for a desire to know God's Word and to share that Truth with people around you. Ask Him to give you a compassionate heart that can be used to steer people toward Truth, and away from wrong thinking and weak beliefs.

PERSONAL EVALUATION

Today I shared with _____

My thoughts on how it went:

_____

_____

_____

_____

What I would do differently?

_____

_____

_____

_____

My prayer for this person?

_____

_____

_____

TRAINING PHASE

4

ONE THING I DO: FORGETTING WHAT IS BEHIND AND STRAINING TOWARD WHAT IS AHEAD, I PRESS ON TOWARD THE GOAL TO WIN THE PRIZE FOR WHICH GOD CALLED ME HEAVENWARD IN CHRIST JESUS
PHIL. 3:13B-14

TRAINING PHASE 4

PRESSING ON

Wow. These past few weeks have been great and hopefully you have learned a lot as you have stepped out in obedience. Remember, we are not gauging success by the number of people you lead to the Lord but by the number of times you are obedient in sharing your story and telling people about the love of Christ.

Just like any physical exercise program, the time comes when you have to decide if you will make the changes permanent—if you will really experience lifestyle change. If not, then you will likely lose the positive ground you have gained. You will be able to remember when "things were different and I felt healthier and stronger" or when "I was living life on the next level"—but we don't want this to be a nice memory for you, we want it to be a reality for you every day!

Please don't let all that God has done in your life through the *21-Day Challenge* be something that you just remember—let it be the way you live life now. Paul said "I press on toward the goal to win the prize." Can you say the same? Are you willing to press on till Jesus comes back? Because that's how long we have to fulfill the purpose for which we were placed here. That's our finish line.

The challenge continues from now—to eternity. The following pages are similar to the ones you have used but they are empty, just waiting for you to allow the Author and Creator of your faith to write the rest of the story. Fill these pages with more and more stories of people you share with and personal evaluations to help you continue growing. You'll be able to look back through these pages and pray over the people you have shared with. When you hear about them accepting Christ and making changes in their lives then record that along with the date.

People in Scripture were continually instructed to put up stones and markers as reminders them of God's faithfulness and His power. This book will be that for you.

Use it as you obey the command of our Lord when He said to 'go and make disciples" so that when that day comes and you stand before a Holy God, you will hear "Well done, good and faithful servant". The finish line is up ahead—keep pressing on!

MY 1 STORY...

Today I shared with _____

MY 1 STORY...

Today I shared with _____

MY 1 STORY...

Today I shared with _____

MY 1 STORY...

Today I shared with _____

MY 1 STORY...

Today I shared with _____

MY 1 STORY...

Today I shared with _____

MY 1 STORY...

Today I shared with _____

MY 1 STORY...

Today I shared with _____

MY 1 STORY...

Today I shared with _____

MY 1 STORY...

Today I shared with _____

MY 1 STORY...

Today I shared with _____

MY 1 STORY...

Today I shared with _____

MY 1 STORY...

Today I shared with _____

MY 1 STORY...

Today I shared with _____

MY 1 STORY...

Today I shared with _____

PRACTICAL HELPS

THE POWER OF 1

EASY TO USE RESOURCES
OFFERING YOU THE PRACTICAL
HELP YOU NEED TO MOST
EFFECTIVELY COMPLETE THE 21
DAY CHALLENGE.

DEVELOPING YOUR STORY

One of the most powerful things you can do in preparing to tell your story is to write it out and think through the different aspects of your relationship with Christ. Use these simple questions to help you organize your thoughts and clarify the story of God's activity in your life.

Sample:
Step One: *Write down what your life was like before you received Christ as your Lord and Savior.*
I grew up in church. However, at the age of seven, my home life took a turn for the worst. My parents were considering divorce. Our home became cold and chaotic. Their problem consumed all of us, and I lost my sense of security.

Step Two: *Share how you came to know and trust Christ*
Because we were still in church, our family decided to attend a crusade with James Robinson. Most of the church members went. I'm glad my family attended. My life was forever changed that night. As I listened, God opened my heart to receive His free gift of love and forgiveness. It was just what my aching heart needed. Therefore, when the evangelist invited all to come forward to receive Christ, I leaped from my chair. My mother followed behind me. That night, I prayed to receive Christ as my Lord and Savior.

Step Three: *Share how your life changed after Christ came into your life.*
Once I received Christ, my problems didn't go away. But, because I had Jesus to lean on, my fears gave way to sweet peace. I knew somehow that whatever happened to my family, I would be more than okay.

Step Four: *Lead them in prayer.*
If you would like to know the peace of Christ, pray this prayer with me: Lord Jesus Christ, I know I am a sinner and do not deserve eternal life. But, I believe You died for me and rose from the grave to purchase a place in heaven for me. Lord Jesus, come into my life and take control; forgive all my sins and save me. I'm turning from my sins and now place my trust in You for my salvation. I accept the free gift of eternal life. Thank you, Jesus for saving me, forgiving me, and filling me with peace. In Jesus name I pray, a-men.

YOUR STORY

Step One:
What my life was like before Jesus:

Step Two:
How I came to realize my need for a Savior:

Step Three:
What my life is like since giving it to Christ:

What God is doing in my life right now:

Each step should be only three to four minutes long so that you easily present your story.

Check out these easy methods that can help steer conversations from the everyday to the eternal. These aren't perfect or all encompassing but they may give you some confidence and spark some other ideas that will work even better as you become more intentional.

1. The Direct Approach

Ask 2 evangelistic questions
1. If you died tonight would you go to heaven?
2. If you did go to heaven and God asked "Why should I let you into my kingdom?", what would you say?

2. Ask about prayer.

In the natural course of your conversation, people will reveal things that could be a concern, issue or problem. When that happens, ask whether they mind if you pray for them. They will possibly ask you about prayer and 'why bother'. That will open the door for you to share about who God is and why it is so comforting and helpful to take burdens to Him. If the conversation doesn't reveal anything more burdensome, then find a way to include some praise to God for how good things are going with them. That will also bring up questions and give you an opportunity to share that "every good and perfect gift is from above" and because of our sinful nature we deserve the worst but God gives us good things.

3. FIRE

A helpful acrostic to get a conversation going in the right direction.
F-friends. Talk about who they know that you may know.
I-interests. Talk about favorite things to do and why they like those.
R-religious background. Talk about way they were raised and if and where they attend church currently.
E-evangelism. Get down to business. Ask if they know what would happen to them if they die today, if they are sure they will go to heaven.

4. Bring Jesus into the conversation.

Find ways to introduce Jesus into any conversation. Talk about something cool you just heard at church, a new song on the radio, last week's sermon topic, anything that you can lead around to who Jesus is to you. Share something that you have recently learned or some exciting way that you had a prayer answered. If you are passionate about the God you serve, people will want to know why and how that can happen. It's contagious.

5. Current Events

As people talk about things that happen in the news, find ways to bring up reliance on God. As you display characteristics of a Christ follower, you may be asked something like "How can you be so peaceful about this terrible economy?" As evil continues to pervade our society there will be more and more opportunities to offer comments about "praying for the people involved in the shooting" and the key to all these conversations goes back to bringing God into it. When they ask why you aren't scared or how you don't panic, tell them your faith is in God alone and He is the only One we can trust. In desperate times, people are more apt to look to the Lord for answers since nothing on this earth is going to give them what they really need. So use these times wisely and speak up.

6. Get them Asking.

Use every method possible to get people to ask you about your faith. If it's a t-shirt with a slogan that creates interest or something from a church event that has a Scripture verse on it, use that for God's glory. Talk about going to Wednesday night services after ball practice and when they ask "why" tell them you need to feed your spirit to keep it healthy during the week. Be willing to refuse to play games during church or practice instead of going to youth camp. Taking a stand and putting your faith first will cause people to start asking questions.

HOW TO SHARE YOUR FAITH

There are lots of different strategies for leading people to surrender their lives to Christ. The key is that you find the way that works best for you and use it. Look through the following examples and try them out until you discover which best fits your personality or situation. REMEMBER: Whatever plan you use, direct people to the Word of God because it has the power to save.

Strategies for leading people to faith in Christ.

1. ABC's of Salvation

A-Admit you're a sinner-Romans 3:23
B-Believe that Jesus died for your sins-John 3:16
C-Confess that you need Jesus to save you from your sin-Romans 10:9-10

2. Share Your Story

—see pages 84-85 for a worksheet to help you develop and organize your own story.

3. Roman Road

Using this strategy, you can walk your friend through the bible verse by verse through the book of Romans.

Romans 5:8, tells us that God loved us so that "when we were in our sin Christ Jesus came to die for us."

Romans 3:23 - "for all have sinned and fall short of the glory of God,"

Romans 6:23 - "For the wages of sin is death, but the free gift of God is eternal life in Christ Jesus our Lord."

Romans 10:9-10 - "that if you confess with your mouth Jesus as Lord, and believe in your heart that God raised Him from the dead, you will be saved; for with the heart a person believes, resulting in righteousness, and with the mouth he confesses, resulting in salvation."

A person receives God's free gift of love and life by placing faith in Jesus Christ. To believe is simply to take God at His word. With our heart (wholly believing) we believe that Jesus is God's Son who died for our sin on the cross and arose from the grave to live in us as Savior and Lord.

To believe in Jesus will result in confessing that faith with one's mouth.
•Do you acknowledge that your are a sinner?
•Do you believe by faith that Jesus, God's Son, died for your sin on the cross?
•Will you now confess Him as your Savior and Lord?

Romans 10:13
"for Whoever will call on the name of the Lord will be saved."

4. Simple Drawing

This is a great outline you can draw in the back of a napkin in a restaurant or envelope at the office.

Step 1. God loves you and has a plan for your life. (John 3:16, John 10:10)

Step 2. Sin is a problem. We all sin. You sin. The cost or wages for sin in our lives in death. (Romans 3;23, Romans 6:23)

Step 3. Draw This:

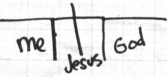

"We can't get to God on our own strength. So Romans 5:8. God sent Jesus to bridge the gap between you and Him."

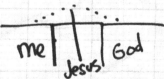

[Draw a cross to connect the 2 cliffs. You might put a stick figure on one side and draw a dotted line showing he crosses over to God's side]

Step 4. Draw a heart. Put some x's in the heart to represent sin in our lives. Draw a square to be the door of your heart and read Revelation 3:20. Say " if you open the door of your heart and let Jesus in then He will wipe away the sin (erase the x's if possible or draw a new, clean heart) and you can be forgiven and made new.

Salvation Prayer

Once you have led someone to the point that they are ready to accept the free gift of salvation, you can give them a simple prayer to pray such as:

> Dear God, I confess that I am a sinner, and I am sorry. I need a Savior. I know I cannot save myself. I believe by faith that Jesus, your son, died on the cross to be my Savior. I believe He arose from the grave to live as my Lord. I turn from my sin. I ask You, Lord Jesus, to forgive my sin and come into my heart. I trust you as my Savior and receive you as my Lord. Thank you, Jesus, for saving me."

What's Next? Congratulate them on their decision and talk to them about next steps of growing in their faith and being baptized. Assure them that they are now a child of the King and nothing or no one can change that. If they have a Bible, encourage them to write their salvation date on the inside cover. If they don't have a Bible, then encourage them to write about this decision along with the date and circumstances somewhere they will see it and be reminded.

To recap:
- •congratulate them
- •encourage them to
    - -write it down
    - -get involved in church
    - -get baptized
    - -tell someone else

IDENTIFYING PEOPLE TO SHARE WITH

How do you go about finding people to talk to about Jesus? Use this cool sketch to help you identify some possible share opportunities in the places you are already involved. The Great Commission tells us to go and make disciples and this worksheet can help you be more intentional about making those disciples 'as you are going' about the places you already frequent.

Write your name in the middle of the circle. Then label each of the spokes with the different places you typically go in a week. (Work, school, neighborhood, ball park, gym, etc) You can add more spokes as necessary.

Next draw lines off each spoke and write the names of people you encounter at each place if you aren't sure of their relationship with Jesus.

This is a great prayer guide for you to use during the **21 Day Challenge**. Keep praying that each of their hearts will be open to the gospel message and that you will have an opportunity to share with them.

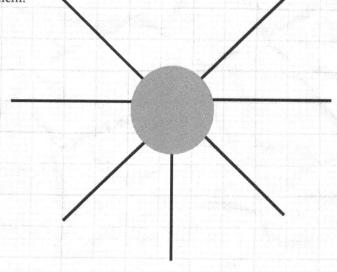

SCRIPTURE MEMORY
... SHARING THE GOSPEL

...for all have sinned and fall short of the glory of God.
Romans 3:23

For the wages of sin is death, but the gift of God is eternal life in Christ Jesus our Lord.
Romans 6:23

But God demonstrates his own love for us in this: While we were still sinners, Christ died for us.
Romans 5:8

This is love: not that we loved God, but that he loved us and sent his Son as an atoning sacrifice for our sins.
1 John 4:10

That if you confess with your mouth, "Jesus is Lord," and believe in your heart that God raised him from the dead, you will be saved.
Romans 10:9

Jesus answered, "I am the way and the truth and the life. No one comes to the Father except through me."
John 14:6

Therefore, there is now no condemnation for those who are in Christ Jesus, because through Christ Jesus the law of the Spirit of life set me free from the law of sin and death.
Romans 8:1

I give them eternal life, and they shall never perish; no one can snatch them out of my hand.
John 10:28

SCRIPTURE MEMORY
... 1 THING YOU MUST DO

There is no fear in love. But perfect love drives out fear...
1 John 4:18

But in your hearts set apart Christ as Lord. Always be prepared to give an answer to everyone who asks you to give the reason for the hope that you have. 1 Peter 3:15

Do nothing out of selfish ambition or vain conceit, but in humility consider others better than yourselves. Each of you should look not only to your own interests, but also to the interests of others.
Philippians. 2:3

For God did not give us a spirit of timidity, but a spirit of power, of love and of self-discipline.
2 Timothy 1:7

But thanks be to God, who always leads us in triumphal procession in Christ and through us spreads everywhere the fragrance of the knowledge of him. 2 Corinthians 2:14

We are therefore Christ's ambassadors, as though God were making his appeal through us. 2 Corinthians 5:20

Am I now trying to win the approval of men, or of God? Or am I trying to please men? If I were still trying to please men, I would not be a servant of Christ. Galatians 1:10

His divine power has given us everything we need for life and godliness through our knowledge of him who called us by his own glory and goodness.
2 Peter 1:3

IF QUESTIONS COME UP...

Many times when you begin a conversation about the faith, people will ask a lot of questions about specific things in their lives. Use this quick reference guide to send them to the Word of God to find answers they seek.

Questions about:

-if Hell is real- Matthew 13:41-42, 25:41; Revelation20:30
-homosexuality-Romans 1:24-27
-premarital sex- 1 Corinthians 6:15-20, Matthew 5:27-32
-drinking 1 Corinthians 5:11, 6:10 and Ephesians 5:18
-unworthy feelings-Colossians 1:13-14, 1 John 1:9, 1 Timothy 2:1-15
-making mistakes- Philippians 3:13, 4:4-7
-anger issues-James 1:19-26, Proverbs 17:34
-gambling-1 Timothy 6:9, Luke 12:15, Proverbs 14:23
-tithe/giving-Hebrews 7:6, Malachi 3:8
-baptism-Matthew 3:13-16,Romans 6:3-8

While this is in no way an exhaustive list, it is a start in directing people to the Word for answers. If a subject comes up that isn't listed, use a search tool from a good online Bible source like:

www.lifeway.com
www.studylight.org
www.mystudybible.com
www.blueletterbible.org

It's OK not to know all the right answers, but definitely share with them that the Bible has all of the answers. Use www.takethe21daychallenge.wordpress.com to share some of the tough questions you encounter. Together we can find the right answers.

FROM THEIR PERSPECTIVE

Have you forgotten what it was like to be the unchurched or lost person? It can be so easy to live in our church world that we forget how to relate to those who aren't where we are. Here you will find some helpful reminders of what to say, what not to say and what that person may be thinking when you share with them. It's good to learn from another's perspective. These are real emotions from people who have come to know Christ but still remember being lost and apart from Him.

1. Don't make me your project. I want to know that you care about me before I want you to share with me. In order to really open doors with me, you have to be willing to invest in the relationship. Don't make me feel like another notch on your spiritual belt.

2. Don't point at me, welcome me. Instead of pointing out all the things that are wrong with my life and the problems I have, accept me as I am.

3. I feel like you are talking down to me when you tell me you will be praying for me. If we are talking and I don't agree with you then don't get up and leave me saying "I'll be praying for you." I don't know your God anyway so when you say that, it makes me feel like you think you're above me. If you want to pray for me then ask me if it's ok, or if there is anything I'd like for you to mention. That comes across much better.

4. I'm watching you. I see how you live. What you dress like. How you act and I listen to the way you talk. If you want me to give any weight to what you have to say about Jesus, then live differently from the world. If you are just like me then why should I go through all the stuff you want me to do about church and God and stuff? We are already exactly the same. Hypocritical behavior is a huge turn off.

5. Don't fake it. I know that you are not perfect, so don't pretend that just because you have 'faith', you have it all together all the time. Everyone messes up and when you admit that to me you seem much more real and your faith is much more attainable. So, don't pretend to be something you aren't. Authenticity is attractive and will lead to evangelism. When I see real people struggle and then walk in faith, it makes me want what you have.